T0209323

WHAT SHOULD YOU DO WITH YOUR LIFE?

Essential Information When
Choosing a Career or Changing One

ISAI REDDY

BALBOA.PRESS

A DIVISION OF HAY HOUSE

Balboa Press books may be ordered through booksellers or by contacting:

Balboa Press
A Division of Hay House
1663 Liberty Drive
Bloomington, IN 47403
www.balboapress.com
844-682-1282

Print information available on the last page.

ISBN: 978-1-9822-5107-9 (sc)
ISBN: 978-1-9822-5106-2 (hc)
ISBN: 978-1-9822-5135-2 (e)

Library of Congress Control Number: 2020913089

Balboa Press rev. date: 08/20/2020

For Tayin and Jaitin Sookan.

Thank you for the ineffable joy and happiness you have brought into our lives.

May your decisions be guided by your higher selves. May you realise and celebrate your hearts' desires with fulfilment and joy, and may you be protected by the higher realms all the days of your lives.

With all my love,
Mum

CONTENTS

INTRODUCTION

Visualise your dream in detail, energize it,
and it will materialize into reality.

Choosing a career might seem like a simple matter of what you enjoy doing or what interests you the most. It is not. In fact, this is an extremely simplified assessment of a complex and life-changing decision. The more time you take and the more key variables you consider, the better will be the final outcome, in terms of personal satisfaction and fulfilment.

This process is one which will significantly impact the rest of your life. It is well worth the effort. It need not necessarily be done at the beginning of one's tertiary academic or post-school stage of life. Although it may save time and disappointment if done at this stage, it could make a crucial impact at any stage. In fact, everyone should do this type of life review and ponder these questions at least every five years, to ensure that one is on the right path to live the best life possible.

There are countless unexpected detours that can send us on seemingly uncontrollable trajectories in our lives. It is of paramount importance to step back and reassess, lest you find yourself in a place you would really rather not be. Furthermore, our ideas, values, and needs are anything but rigid and static. We change as we grow and interact with the world. Life happens and expectations change. In fact, the whole point of living is to learn and grow spiritually, so it's only natural that your thoughts and expectations are very different at 40 years of age compared to 20 years. Some people are fortunate enough to understand themselves and choose their careers suitably right off the bat, but we aren't all so lucky. Lack of opportunities, financial restrictions and other factors may keep some from pursuing their heart's desire early in life.

If you do have financial commitments and responsibilities—such as student loans, a home bond, or indigent parents—these may take priority, as well they should! You may need to work and take care of these obligations first. The important principle to always remember is that you must have a plan. Perhaps your plan could be to work hard and pay off your debts, establish a home for your family, and educate the kids, then go full steam ahead with your dream.

If this is the route you are on, the crucial make-or-break variable is to not shackle yourself with material things. Once you are earning, the temptation can be overwhelming to indulge in an expensive house, sports cars, or golf memberships in upmarket country clubs. You must be absolutely honest with yourself and steadfast in your beliefs and dreams. Constantly remind yourself of what the plan is. Keep the vision alive in your mind. Do not waver and get distracted, or you will be lost.

You may think at some point, 'Why should I chase my dreams if this job is paying the bills and giving me a comfortable life?' My perspective on this is that the empty fulfilment and thrill you receive from acquisitions will diminish with time. As you get older, in all likelihood, you will want a more meaningful life. The career you settled for may start to frustrate you and make you resentful. If you keep working towards your dream, you can enjoy the benefits of the current, lucrative job and still invest in your soul purpose and future happiness. Don't settle for the consolation prize when you can have the jackpot.

One of the benefits of yoga and meditation is precisely to slow down the often frenetic pace of life, at least for a few moments each day, so that you may gain some perspective and insight into your own personal journey in this lifetime and get some direction. It will also help you maintain perspective and keep true to the path you have envisioned for yourself.

Nothing is cast in stone, and you can always change careers if you choose to. It would, however, save you a lot of time, money, and inconvenience to choose wisely and more appropriately from the start, if you are privileged enough to have that opportunity.

It becomes more difficult to change careers once you have children and other commitments. The last thing you want at this stage is to be stuck in a job or career that you don't like and are unhappy with, just because you need it to pay your bills. This is the trap of our century and best avoided if possible.

The purpose of this book is to help you choose as appropriately as possible at this stage of your life. If you consider all the variables mentioned here carefully and honestly, you will make the best decision for you at this point in time. Even if you do change later on, at least you know that this was an informed, well-deliberated move that was in your best interest at the time.

Also, remember always that ultimately no education is ever wasted. It is incorporated into all facets of our lives and is part of our soul's journey. Knowledge is always worth acquiring.

Disclaimer

Please note that if you are not financially independent and are relying on others to support you, the priority for you may be to get a job—any respectable paying job—to become financially independent. If your dream job is not immediately possible, that is fine. Once you are on your feet and able to support yourself, you can plan your perfect life. Studying part-time while working is often an option.

Do not for a second believe that I am in any way suggesting that you should rely on someone else for your upkeep while you are chilling and holding out for the ideal dream job or career. If you are straight out of school and your parents are supporting you through your studies, that's fine. If you are 28 years old and waiting around for your dream job, that is not acceptable by any stretch of the imagination. If this is your position, please get off your ass and get a job!

CHAPTER 1
IT'S YOUR DECISION

This above all—to thine own self be true,
And it must follow, as the night the day,
Thou can'st not then be false to any man.
—William Shakespeare, *Hamlet*

Whatever you decide about your career, please ensure that it is your decision. This may seem simple enough, but it isn't—not at a stage in your life when so much is uncertain (if you've just finished school). There are so many options and so many influential factors. As difficult as it may be, you have to try to shut out the noise, which may be of varying intensity. Here I'm referring to parental and societal pressure, peer pressure, and your perceptions of what is expected of you and of what you think your aptitude is based on scholastic performance. Remember that as much as others may want what they think is best for you, no one is in your mind and feels exactly what you do. It has to be your decision.

You must also understand and accept that ultimately you bear the responsibility for whatever decisions you make. Later on in life, you cannot blame someone else for your choices, and even if you do, what would be the point so long after the fact? Although outside influences may be strong and persuasive, we cannot blame others for our decisions, which we have the free will to change at any point in time.

Remember that you are an adult now, and when it comes to your life, you have to be strong and assertive if necessary. Learn to identify manipulative behaviour from family and friends. Also try to understand that sometimes our elders mean well but may be speaking from limited life experience or knowledge of the opportunities available. In these cases, you have to first understand their perspective and yours. You have to stand your ground, but in doing so, try to be sensitive to their feelings.

Try to make them see why this is a good choice for you. Perhaps explain what your proposed career is all about, and expose them to it if possible. You could show them someone successful in the field. This will help them feel more secure in your choice. Those who truly care for you will want you to be happy and not push a personal agenda. Sometimes they don't see the full picture, and you have to be compassionate. Being compassionate is not capitulating to pressure. You also have a duty to yourself.

It is very difficult to give the best of yourself to the world, including your family, if you are miserable and frustrated. Your career or job will consume a large portion of your life. Don't take it lightly. Many young people have suffered serious depression, and some have even resorted to desperate measures to get out of a soul-destroying career, including something as noble and respected as medicine. We are all unique, and what works for one person may not necessarily work for another. Get to know yourself and who you are. I will try to help you do this.

If you feel a strong need to fulfil your parents' wishes in following a path that they have chosen, that's okay. Once again, it's entirely your decision. Similarly, if you feel the need to stay close to home— for example, due to elderly or ill parents—that is your choice, but you need to own it. You cannot and should not be resentful at a later stage because of this choice.

It is perfectly fine to not follow your first choice at the beginning, but make sure you understand and accept this decision. You can still plan ahead. For example, you can take courses that will build up to what you ultimately want to do or that will enhance your knowledge or experience for the future. Richard Branson worked in sales, gaining incredible knowledge and perspective in business, before embarking on what is now one of the most iconic business success stories of all time. All business ultimately comes down to selling people things, so he enhanced his basic skills and built on that.

It all starts with what makes you tick. So let's figure that out, shall we?

PERSONAL NOTES

PERSONAL NOTES

CHAPTER 2
WHAT DO YOU ABSOLUTELY HATE DOING?

> Happiness is when what you think, what you
> say, and what you do are in harmony.
> —Mahatma Gandhi

So, let's get started on discovering the best path for you. A good place to begin is to consciously consider all the things in life that just don't gel with you. This will range from *definitely no way*, to *I don't think so*, to *maybe*.

We are talking about spending the majority of your waking hours each day embroiled in an activity. It has to be something you are comfortable doing, or you will be miserable. There are more than enough career options out there, so you should never feel limited or pressured into choosing something that you don't particularly like. Every person on this planet has a special attribute. If you can figure out what that is for you, life will be effortless, at least in terms of your work.

To begin, make a list of all the things you really do not like to do. Then jot down what fields each may eliminate from consideration. Here are some examples:

- cannot tolerate blood → exclude nursing, medical doctor, paramedic
- hate working with computers → exclude IT (although you may have to make some effort with the computers, as it is the way of the world)

- do not like working with numbers → exclude accounting, actuarial science
- do not like talking to people → exclude sales, teaching

How you relate to authority will also impact your career pathway. This overlaps with the chapter on personal expectations and boundaries. If you absolutely hate being told what to do, you may have to think in terms of being an independent practitioner of some sort or perhaps opening your own business. Self-employment would be the preferred option.

Once you have done the first draft of this list, leave at least two blank pages to add to it as thoughts and ideas pop up along the way.

Next, make a list of your preferred career options at this stage—the more, the better. Once you have the list, go through each of the job descriptions carefully. Correlate this with your disfavoured list. Use a highlighter or a different brightly coloured pen to flag the ones that clash. In this way, you should be able to eliminate some of the less-suitable options. At the very least, you will be more aware of and cautious about these paths.

If you are not entirely familiar with what a particular job or career entails, please try to find out everything you can. Read about it, talk to people in the field, and try to spend time observing what really happens on a realistic, practical level. The theory can often be very different from the actual job. A job can be fascinating from an academic point of view, but the practicalities involved in actually doing the work may not be as agreeable. Please be careful not to be mesmerized by the image or lifestyle you perceive a career will offer you. This will wear off very quickly.

These lists are not meant to be static or rigid in any way. Keep them safe, with plenty of room for additions, notes, alterations, and so on. Add to them whenever necessary. Preferably, keep all these notes in a book. You may need it again later in life.

Whatever you do, please do not force yourself into a career that you know is not for you just to please others. People who care about you will never want you to be miserable, so be honest about your personal boundaries—to yourself and the significant people in your life. This is your life. The sooner you own it, the sooner you will start to flourish and enjoy the journey.

PERSONAL NOTES

PERSONAL NOTES

CHAPTER 3
WHAT MAKES YOU HAPPY?

Choose a job you love. And you will never
have to work a day in your life.
—attributed to Confucius

I could have titled this chapter 'What do you enjoy doing?' or 'What are your strengths and talents?' I chose 'What makes you happy?' because this is more instinctive—it is the deep-rooted, heart-warming, gut-instinct response I am looking for. Speak from your soul.

To do this, you need to try to ignore and let go of your ego's needs, people's expectations of you, and your desire to fulfil an image. For example, you may like the look and appeal of being a doctor with a stethoscope around your neck, but you cannot handle blood or touching people. Take as much time as you need to meditate, ponder the possibilities, and be alert to what makes your pulse race (with excitement—not fear). What makes you smile and feels most natural to you?

Now write down all the things you enjoy doing, such as travelling, cooking, reading, or computer work. Then make a list of all the career options that are possible with these key variables. Flag any aspects of the job that don't appeal to you. This may only be possible after research.

At this stage, you have to be proactive like never before. Use every avenue of research to investigate each of your career options. Watch videos on YouTube; search the Internet; speak to teachers at school and friends of your parents; and contact relevant companies. Try to spend time with professionals in your chosen field. Make appointments to see and talk to them. Try to get a holistic view of their lives. Familiarise yourself with a typical day in their lives.

For example, a salon owner may spend part of the day meeting with representatives and suppliers, planning advertisements, and troubleshooting staff issues. Imagine yourself doing these things. How does it make you feel? This is of paramount importance in any field you choose. Reality can be quite different from your perception of what the job entails.

Ask individuals in your field of interest if you can observe them at work. If possible, speak to more than one person to get a less biased view. Make sure you are prepared with your list of questions covering everything you need to know. Try not to waste time on basics that you can pick up from the Internet and other easily accessible sources. Focus on pertinent aspects that are of concern to you personally and those aspects that you are uncertain or confused about.

Remember to find out about promotions and opportunities for career advancement. How far or high can this take you, financially and in terms of personal fulfilment? Imagine yourself doing this for many years. How does that make you feel? Would you be content to be in the same position for however many years it takes to advance up the ladder?

Once you have spent time researching and doing fieldwork, go back to your list. Draw a table with three columns as indicated.

Career Option	Pros	Cons
Hairdresser	Creative, meet many people	On your feet all day
Journalist	Travel, exciting	Can be dangerous
Nurse	Get to help sick people	Terrible working hours in training and junior positions

Fill it in as honestly as possible. The longer your points, the better for you.

Leave enough space, perhaps one page, for each potential career. Keep going back to the list as your knowledge and understanding of the field increases. You will also need to go back to the list once you contemplate factors discussed in the chapters that follow, including how you relate to authority, working hours, protocols (like clocking in and out), and parental expectations.

Please also consider that some less-appealing aspects of training may be temporary. One example might be the late hours required when training to be a nurse. Once you qualify, you can choose a job with normal daylight hours. I had to do fifty post mortems (autopsies) as part of my training to be an anatomical pathologist, but once I qualified, I didn't have to do them anymore. Only you can decide if any sacrifice is worth it in the long run, so think about it carefully. If some part of a job makes you extremely uncomfortable and stresses you out, it is most likely not worth it.

I strategically positioned this chapter in the beginning so that you can become more aware of your personal proclivities as you read the other chapters. You can then come back and fill in these work pages.

Let me reiterate that work need not be a chore. Yes, perhaps we might all be happiest with a big trust fund and lives of pure leisure and luxury, but that isn't possible for most of us. Why not carve out a path of fulfilment, accomplishment, and joyful contribution to the world?

We are sometimes unfortunately conditioned by watching the adults around us struggle with hardship and toil in their careers. Do not let this build up an image of work as a constant uphill battle of drudgery and misery. You must hold on steadfastly to your own imagery of personal fulfilment, joy, and ease.

PERSONAL NOTES

PERSONAL NOTES

CHAPTER 4

PERSONAL EXPECTATIONS AND BOUNDARIES: TIME VERSUS MONEY WHERE DO YOU DRAW THE LINE?

What is this life if, full of care,
We have no time to stand and stare.
    … … … …
No time to see, when woods we pass,
Where squirrels hide their nuts in grass.
No time to see, in broad daylight,
Streams full of stars, like skies at night.
    … … …
A poor life this if, full of care,
We have no time to stand and stare.
—'Leisure', William Henry Davies

When you're young and life is relatively uncomplicated, you may not recognize your expectations and personal boundaries. These only become apparent when you are challenged.

For example, you may exercise four times a week, for two-hour sessions each time. This is what you do and what you need in your life to keep fit, healthy, and feeling good. You take it for granted that it's just the way life is—until you start working twelve hours a day and are exhausted at the end of the day. You just can't exercise. Perhaps you have children to care for after your workday ends. When do you exercise, read or whatever it is that you look forward to at the end of the day?

Insidiously, this new lifestyle starts to eat at your soul. This is when you realise what your boundaries are. You think, 'I did not sign up for this!'

What is it that you are simply not prepared to compromise on in your life? It could be anything. Please note that nobody can tell you that it's not important. Only you know what's important to you. To presume that this key activity or pastime is not of value is sheer arrogance on the part of anyone telling you so.

For me, running, reading, and quality time with my children are most important. For you, it could be anything—dancing, fishing, watching movies. If it's important to you and helps keep you balanced in this world, you shouldn't have to give it up. This is real life. Work will have its merits, but it is extremely dangerous in the long run if it keeps you from the things you enjoy in life.

I sincerely believe that alcohol abuse, smoking, even extramarital affairs would be significantly reduced if people were happier and spent more time feeding their souls, not just their wallets. On the other hand, maybe you are a workaholic. If that is what makes you happy beyond all else in life, then that's just fine.

The essence of this discussion is: Do you want a career that gives you a balance—that is, work satisfaction and quality personal time—or do you not mind a career that is all-consuming? There are people who are so passionate about their job that they do not mind it being all-consuming. We do not judge. Hopefully, it's not hurting anyone else.

I have given up the chance to work towards partnership in a big company because it compromised my time with my children, and consumed far more of my time and energy than I was willing to give. The demands of the job and the expectations of the company were also beginning to erode my soul. The environment was too toxic and restricting for me.

This is a very personal variable and choice. No one can tell you what should be important to you. You have to be completely honest with yourself about your limitations and needs.

Please also always weigh the risks. Do not make hasty, irrational decisions. You need to have a plan and a safety net. Do not give up a secure job without thinking carefully about your options. This is why it is so important to know yourself. Many people try to tolerate a soul-destroying job or career by rationalizing the benefits, be it monetary or otherwise. This is dangerous because when they reach their limit, they may not be able to make a calculated move, and it ends with an explosive crisis rather than a well-thought-out plan of action.

The following are some other variables to consider:

- How do you feel about being limited by times—such as 8 a.m. to 5 p.m.—and having your work hours monitored? Can you handle this, or would you prefer completely flexible hours? Perhaps you could compromise and tolerate the restrictions as a junior with the knowledge that it will be better when you are senior.
- Can you handle working night shifts, or do you need normal daylight hours? How do you feel about overtime?
- How do you relate to authority? Can you handle people telling you what to do, or would you rather be your own boss—working for a company compared to running your own business? Once again, perhaps you could gain experience as an employee before going out on your own. Planning is everything.
- Can you work in an office all day, or would you prefer to travel about in your job? Are you claustrophobic? Are there any aspects of the job that may be a problem in this regard?
- Would you prefer to be able to delegate some or most of your duties to junior staff in the future, or do you enjoy a job that requires your full attention and effort? This is important because some jobs just can't be delegated ever. If you are a surgeon, for example, no one else can do the operation, unless you hire a locum.

- Would you like to be in charge someday, as a CEO or a manager? Is there scope for this in the job you are considering?
- How important are your hobbies, such as sport, hiking, or yoga? How would you feel if work imposed on these or prevented you from doing them entirely? If there are activities that are vital to your core being and personal sanity, you need a job that allows you the time and energy to enjoy your activity of choice.

Your personal boundaries may change as you go through life. This is completely natural, since our lives are not static. As our circumstances and priorities change, so do our expectations and limitations. Don't be afraid to analyse your situation and reassess every few years or as life dictates.

Remember always that this is your life. You can't blame others at the end of it for the choices you have made. This is an extremely important aspect of planning your life. Only you can do it properly.

PERSONAL NOTES

PERSONAL NOTES

CHAPTER 5
APTITUDE VERSUS PERSONAL CHOICE

Two roads diverged in a wood, and I –
I took the one less travelled by,
And that has made all the difference.
—'The Road Not Taken', Robert Frost

Just because you are intelligent does not mean that you have to do what all intelligent people are doing in your circle, such as seeking careers in medicine or aeronautical engineering. Just because you can do it and are chosen over and above everyone else to do so, does not mean that you should.

Remember, work is not like studying. When you are studying, everything is new, exciting, and challenging. However, most jobs entail doing the same thing every day, to varying degrees. This could become extremely monotonous, and frustrating if you don't really enjoy what you're doing. Try to envision yourself doing it every day, year in and year out.

Yes, you can change careers. This is always an option, so it is never all doom and gloom. There are always options. The difficulty is that after you've invested time, effort, and money into a career, it becomes less easy to leave. Furthermore, once you start earning, chances are you will incur some financial obligations—such as a house, car, and children's school fees—which will have to be met. Changing careers, and possibly starting at the bottom again, will not be so easy, emotionally, physically, or financially. Some careers, such as commerce, are more versatile, with many possible options when you get to the top. Others, such as medicine and paramedical specialties (optometry, physiotherapy) are not.

Putting in the effort to see what your heart and soul truly desire at the outset is therefore time well invested. Look at every option holistically, not just in terms of monetary gain or status. You are a holistic being with many facets. Try to choose in a way that will please all aspects of you. You will be a much happier and peaceful human being if you do. This will benefit everyone around you, especially your family and close friends.

PERSONAL NOTES

PERSONAL NOTES

CHAPTER 6
THE ACTUAL STUDYING

When you do things from your soul, you
feel a river moving in you, a joy.
—Rumi

Deciding what it is you want to study is just the first step. Yet it is a monumental decision, as we have established, and of profound importance. Once you have decided, you need to familiarise yourself with the programme.

We may have covered some of this when discussing aspects of a particular job that may not be appealing to you. Some academic programmes do include practical work. The actual curriculum might also be a problem. Before investing time, money, and emotion, it would be wise to see what is in store for you.

Contact the relevant university or tertiary institution and find out who you can speak to in your chosen department. In addition, get a detailed course outline and requirements. You should also speak to students in the programme, preferably one or two from each year of study, to get a comprehensive idea of the course.

The following are some of the questions you'll want to ask:

- How much study time is required? This is the personal time invested aside from formal lectures and practical sessions. Please note that this usually differs from one year of study to the next.
- How much group work is involved, and how intensely do you all need to work together?

- How often are tests, examinations, oral assessments, and presentations done?
- Are students required to travel? If so, is transport provided?
- Are there any additional costs or expenses that a prospective student needs to be aware of?

Please make your own list of details as you become aware of them. Take note of information that is relevant to your specific academic programme and of interest to you personally. You need to assess whether these requirements and expectations of you are realistic, in terms of your own personal limitations and abilities. If you have young children or other important responsibilities that occupy a lot of your time, it may be better for you to study part-time. There is no one-size-fits-all where these aspects of life are concerned. Your plans need to be bespoke to accommodate your individual idiosyncrasies and needs.

Only you can understand what will be best for you. Planning your career path well saves you time, money, and heartache. You can still become a successful accountant if you study part-time. Don't compromise the things that are important to you for some perceived expectations. Life won't sit around and wait until you are ready to pick up again, especially if you have a young family.

If there are aspects of the training that you just can't handle, you need to decide if it's worth the effort and struggle. Can you do it without traumatising yourself excessively? Once again, only you can know this. Sometimes you can only know the answer once you give it a try. There is nothing wrong with that. You can always stop and change course.

PERSONAL NOTES

PERSONAL NOTES

CHAPTER 7
EXTRACURRICULAR ACTIVITIES

> True wisdom comes to each of us when we
> realise how little we understand about life,
> ourselves, and the world around us.
> —Socrates

Any type of studying can be emotionally draining and sometimes physically exhausting. You will need time to relax and unwind. This applies to school as well as tertiary education and even your working life thereafter. It is imperative to unwind and relax; however, how you do so is also important. Some methods may not really help ultimately and may even tire you more.

The television, Internet, and devices such as PlayStation are particularly easily accessible and tempting. Please be very careful. If you spend a lot of time staring at a computer screen, staring at another screen is not going to help your body and mind relax in the ways it needs.

Electronic devices drain your energy and strain your eyes. It is perfectly fine to indulge yourself for a bit to get your mind off work, but please don't let it suck up all your time and energy. It is not a productive way to spend free time.

We are all addicted to the Internet. My personal vice is Candy Crush (a game on mobile phones and notebooks). I can play for hours. The problem is that if we are not making enough time for exercise, fresh air, and soul-fulfilling activities, we are doing ourselves a disservice and endangering our health.

Please try to make time for sport and exercise, perhaps walking, hiking, or running. Make sure it is somewhere safe. Also ensure that you get enough sleep. Never underestimate the value of restful sleep, not only on your academic performance but on your quality of life in general.

What about spending time with friends and family? This is a very personal decision. Some people feel totally relaxed and uplifted after going out, or spending time at family functions. Others may feel drained, irritated, and uninspired, to say the least. This one is your call. If you have a great time out with friends and family, that is wonderful. Enjoy every moment. Just remember to keep it in perspective. As long as your studies are on track and you are not compromising your career, there should be no problem.

If, however, some of these groups have a negative effect on you, avoid contact. It will only waste your precious time and upset you. Avoid negative people—those who are spiteful, jealous, pessimistic, egomaniacal, or just have impure intentions towards you. You need to protect your space and peace of mind; forcefully if necessary. Set your boundaries and protect them. Protect your health.

Avoid Energy Vampires! You Need Good Vibes!

Alcohol and drugs—need I really discuss these? I'm sure you know that these are hollow and destructive indulgences. Occasional alcohol in small quantities, preferably with company, may seem innocuous enough. Do not let it become a habit, however; do not crave it, and most certainly do not rely on it to relax you or to give yourself confidence. This behaviour will destroy you in the long run.

No amount of rationalisation will suffice. Drugs? Just don't go there, please. Nothing good can ever come of it. It is not cool in any way. Anyone who encourages you to indulge in these activities, is not your friend.

Yoga and meditation are the way of the future. These activities will help you relax your body, mind, and soul, and energise you in many ways. You may feel that you simply do not have the time.

Make the time. Just a few minutes a day will be well worth it. Make it a routine and part of your daily schedule, like brushing your teeth or having a shower. Just a few minutes a day will have profound long-term benefits.

PERSONAL NOTES

PERSONAL NOTES

CHAPTER 8
KEEPING IT IN PERSPECTIVE

Life is really simple, but we insist
on making it complicated.
—Confucius

Yes, indeed, choosing a career path is important. It will have a major impact on your future life. However it is not the most important thing in your life. Remember that. The most important thing in your life is your health and well-being—physical, emotional, and spiritual. Do not let any person, thing, or situation compromise your health and sanity. Nothing is worth that much.

Your job is just a job—something that you do for money and, if you choose wisely, for fun, enjoyment and personal fulfillment. People change careers all the time. People from all socioeconomic backgrounds and all education levels, even after years of investment in a particular field, find new options.

It is of paramount importance to have peace of mind. When you are studying, plan yourself well, so that you do as much as is realistically possible. Remember that no two people study the same way. Do what works for you, and do not try to follow someone else's routine or study programme. You must devise one that is individualistic, just for you.

Use the following questions to guide you in planning your studies or drawing up a study timetable:

- *How many hours can you study before needing a break?* Bear in mind that this needs to be flexible and based on the particular subject matter. You may be able to effortlessly put in long hours if it's your favourite subject. If, on the other hand, it is something you struggle with or find rather taxing, you may need shorter sessions to be able to focus.

- *How long are your breaks?* Frequent short breaks are advisable to refresh your mind and rest your eyes. Longer breaks can be taken every two hours or so, depending on your personal needs. You can try different intervals and duration of breaks and see what works best for you.

- *How much sleep do you need?* Do not deprive yourself of sleep, and please do not compare yourself to other people. If you need six hours, take it. Factor this into your study timetable/plan so that you cover all relevant course material in the time you have.

- *Are you eating properly?* Please do not diet while studying, especially Carbohydrate free diets. Your brain needs sugar, so don't deprive it and then expect to perform well. Eat normal, well-balanced meals.

- *Are you getting enough exercise?* Exercise is a source of stress relief and relaxation. It boosts blood circulation, which improves oxygen supply to all your tissues, including your brain. Get into a good routine long before examinations and try to maintain it. If you are a fitness fanatic, you might need to cut out a few sessions to make time for studying. If you hardly ever exercise, please do not start a strenuous routine just before exams. Your body and mind need to be relaxed and active, not totally exhausted or sluggish. Get a good balance well before you start seriously studying so it will be part of your routine and not a shock to the system.

- *When should you study: day or night?* Study when you are most productive and can benefit the most. This is entirely dependent on you.

- *What music helps you study?* Music can be therapeutic and therefore very helpful. If you enjoy a certain type, make sure you listen to it often to help you relax. I used to listen to Kenny G before every exam.

- The idea is to plan well. Do as much as you can: emphasis here is on *you*. If you are working all day, there is only so much time you can allocate to studies at night. That is something you need to accept and factor into your timetable. If you do as much as you can, then it has to be enough. At that point, leave it to the higher powers to guide you.

If your paper does not go as planned, please do not stress over it. Use it as a learning experience for next time. See where and how you can improve and make a note of it. Then move on. It's over. There is no point whatsoever in obsessing about it. Rather, focus on the rest of the exam.

Remember, whatever happens, it is just your studies. There was a life before this, and there will be one after, irrespective. Do your best. That's all you can do.

PERSONAL NOTES

PERSONAL NOTES

CHAPTER 9
THE REST OF YOUR LIFE

*May you have the courage and confidence
to respect and honour who you are and
what you need from this world.*

Take a moment, preferably many, to ponder your expectations of life with regard to marriage, a life partner, and children—essentially, family life. What do you envisage for yourself? This is extremely important for many reasons. We often believe, albeit subconsciously, that once we get our careers sorted, the rest will fall into place. We will meet the perfect partner and ride off into the sunset. We have worked so hard, after all. Surely this part will be easy. Maybe it will be; however, more often than not, this needs to be carefully considered.

You have a much better chance of a happy life with a partner, married or not, if you are honest with yourself and that partner about your needs and expectations. Please do not be shy. Remember, again, it is your life. You know best what you need out of it. It is going to be your family, not your friends', not your mum's or dad's.

You will have to take responsibility for your family. You cannot be the best partner or parent you can be if you make decisions that compromise your needs. You are *not* being selfish! You are being responsible. You are showing trust and respect by being honest about who you really are.

Our generation is capable of so much. We have the ability to accomplish just about anything we want. My experience and observations have been that those individuals who have a clear idea of who they are and what they want out of life get exactly that. It's a question of self-confidence and standing up for yourself. If you doubt yourself for whatever reason (overcritical parents or teachers, tough childhood, poor academic performance), please work on it. You are worthy of a great life: the exact one that you deserve.

In, fact the tougher your childhood, the more you have to offer the world. You may have a greater degree of empathy and a greater capacity for understanding and compassion compared to someone who has grown up without challenges, emotional or financial. Whoever you are, you have special talents that the world needs. Don't deprive our world of all you can offer. It's your time. Grab it.

If you need some therapy for emotional issues from childhood, go for it. Maybe you need time out in a Buddhist retreat for a few months (boy, could I have done with this in my younger days—how I wish). Please make the time and do it. Anyone who truly cares about the real you will support you. In this life, no one really matters other than those who truly care about the real you, not their version of who you should be.

Some of the aspects of adult life that you should clarify in your mind are as follows:

1. What are your expectations regarding roles and responsibilities in the home—housework, cooking, buying groceries, caring for the children, school pick-ups, and the like? If you believe these should be shared, please make this known to your partner. Don't take it for granted that this is how it will be. It does not work that way in the real world. You do not have superpowers. If both partners intend to work, these responsibilities will be extremely challenging to do all on one's own.

2. Do you intend to have domestic help? How much? A nanny for your children?

3. Does your partner expect you to be a stay-at-home parent? Do they believe it is their responsibility to share all these activities or do they feel that they will be doing you a favour

by 'helping' you? There is a big difference. When work gets challenging, your partner can't drop the ball and expect you to just be available—unless this is acceptable to you.

4. What are your plans regarding the future—studying, work travel, and leisure travel? Do you want to see the world? Will you look for opportunities to work and travel abroad? Please discuss these plans. If there is something you have always dreamed about doing, you should not abandon that possibility unless you are absolutely certain. It will help to know where you stand and what your options are. Apparently, not everyone believes travelling around the world is a great idea.

   Also, please bear in mind that this will not be easy or even possible at all once you have children. Everything changes. You should get your wanderlust sorted, fed, and satisfied as much as possible before your babies arrive. You will be a much better parent if you are not restless and yearning for personal adventure and excitement.

5. How much time and space do you need for yourself? Make this very clear from the start. Does your partner expect you to spend every weekend with family or friends? Your personal space is something sacred. It is your time to recharge, recuperate, and re-energise yourself. Defend it with all you have. It is soul food, and is very important to your well-being. It doesn't matter what you choose to do with it. Meditate, read, watch television, relax in a spa— whatever you do is your business, and if it's important to you, the person closest to you must respect it.

As much as you do not want to burden a relationship with these considerations, there will come a time when you are contemplating a serious commitment to someone. These issues could place considerable strain on a marriage. At the very least, you need to know what you are getting into. Do not assume anything. Addressing these aspects of life early on could save you a lot of pain in the future.

We are all exposed to stereotypes of one form or another. We grow up watching our parents take on certain roles. Families sometimes indoctrinate you with their ideas. Our young, innocent, vulnerable minds often incorporate some of these ideas into our subconscious.

For example, one might believe that a good wife should always cook and do the dishes irrespective of her own personal challenges (work, a difficult day with the children, and so on). This is not true! Please banish it from your mind. When reality hits, you will become extremely frustrated because your education and personal beliefs will conflict with subconscious ideas. You should decide for yourself what you need to do, not dogmatically adhere to unrealistic, prehistoric notions of womanhood.

On the other hand, guys may feel pressurized to be the breadwinner, due to old fashioned subconscious beliefs. Many families, these days, work better with the women at work and the husbands at home with the kids. Once again, it is personal preferences and what works in your home. Do not disadvantage yourselves due to primitive beliefs.

Your choice of career as well, should not be influenced by your gender. Men are doing phenomenally well at careers like hairdressing, dress designing and nursing. It is who you are as an individual, and no one really knows that better than you.

There seems to be in some quarters a misconception about 'having it all'. What exactly does this mean? If it means having a high-powered job, raising your kids, and running around participating in a million other socially enviable activities, then personally I would say 'no thank you'. That's just my subjective point of view. You must decide what having a good life means to you. Don't bother about what everyone else is doing. I will elaborate more on the challenges and joys of being a parent in the next chapter.

Ultimately, we are all wonderfully unique. Your happiness in this lifetime depends on you. Only you can truly know what is in your heart. Take the time to know yourself. May you find a partner who understands who you are and respects your needs. More importantly, may you have the courage and confidence to respect and honour who you are and what you need from this world, with or without a partner.

PERSONAL NOTES

PERSONAL NOTES

CHAPTER 10
CHILDREN AND YOUR CAREER

Warmth is the vital element for the growing
plant, and for the soul of the child.
—Carl Jung

Children, to me, are the most precious, pure, and beautiful beings. We are so blessed to have them in our world. Being a parent is the ultimate honour and privilege. These are souls who have chosen us to be their parents.

Having children should not be something you do because that's what everyone does or says you should do. You should not have children because you are afraid there will be no one to care for you in your old age. Hopefully, your children will not be unwanted products of a lustful relationship.

So then, what exactly do *you* think about being a parent? If you are a healthy human being, this is something you need to think about *now*, not when it happens!

How important is it to you to have children? Do you even want to have children? Please discuss this with your partner, if you have one. Both your views and feelings are so very important. If your partner is adamant about not wanting to have children, this is also important. Don't brush it off, believing your partner will have a change of mind when the time is right. Chances are, that will not happen. Most people who do not want children have very good reasons for feeling this way. Often, there are deeply entrenched beliefs and emotions. It is not a whimsical notion. You must respect that and accept it, even if it means the two of you may not have a future together. It's every individual's choice and prerogative.

Once you decide that you do want kids (if you don't, well and good and off you go), consider carefully what kind of parent you would like to be. Let me assure you, whatever it is you have in mind now, it will be so much more intense once that child is in your arms. I always knew that I wanted to be a mum, but I could not have imagined in my wildest dreams what it would mean for me as an independent career woman. It truly did turn my life upside down.

There is absolutely nothing that I wouldn't do for the well-being of my children. I do not believe in regrets. There is no point, because you can't go back and change anything. That said, there are certainly things and choices I would change had I known what it would feel like to be a mum.

I am not in any way suggesting that you lower your ambitions on account of wanting to be a parent. On the contrary, you simply need to plan properly so that you are in a position of greater autonomy, with more options. The idea of aftercare, nannies, caregivers, and other helpers is a lot more appealing to some parents than others. It is, of course, entirely your choice.

Being a stay-at-home parent or a half-day working parent is an option not available to many, as the cost of raising children is quite high. School fees alone necessitate two working parents in many instances. In order to stay fulfilled in your job and not grow to resent it, it is important to firstly choose the right career path and secondly be where you want to be positioned in that career hierarchy when your children do come along.

Once again, discuss your parenting roles and responsibilities with your partner. If you are a woman, you should not have to compromise your career if your partner can meet you halfway. This is something very personal, and only you and your partner can decide what works for you. Whatever decision you make, as long as you are happy and comfortable with it, that is fine. It is no one else's business anyway.

Choosing to take time out of your career to devote to the children, whether you are male or female, is a noble, loving decision.

I do not believe that it is one you will ever regret. Like I said, children are precious, and they grow up so fast. Cherishing every moment of their childhood as much as you can is something you will be so grateful for when they are all grown up and don't really need you that much anymore.

PERSONAL NOTES

PERSONAL NOTES

CHAPTER 11
HEALTH AND CAREER

Beware the barrenness of a busy life.
—Socrates

Your chosen career will inevitably, profoundly, impact your health and well-being in many ways. Unfortunately, many people realise this too late in their lives and careers. They get swept up in the corporate whirlwind, busy trying to establish their careers and meet soaring financial commitments.

There is often the misperception of 'I will address this health issue as soon as I get that promotion, my kids are older, I pay off my home bond' and so on. Needless to say, this is often too late. It is tragic how many people work their asses off their entire lives and wait expectantly for their well-earned retirement, only to die before it comes or soon after.

Once you start working, free time becomes a precious, elusive commodity. Waking up at 4 or 5 a.m. to run or go to the gym before work is not so easy when you are working late hours and/or are the parent of an infant or toddler. Being healthy is a combination of attitude, genetics, exercise, getting enough relaxation, eating well, and any other factor that impacts your emotional or physical state. Never-ending deadlines and a heavy workload can place considerable demands on a person. This can lead to irritability, compromise crucial relationships, and leave very little time to exercise or prepare healthy meals. It does also, unfortunately, in many cases contribute to people turning to alcohol, drugs, smoking, and the like to cope or escape from their unbearably stressful lives.

So what should you do? Go through the following steps:

1. When you think of your career choice, picture yourself doing exactly what it is that you love doing (after making a list of your first three choices with all the pros and cons).

2. Think about how you would like your life to be, holistically, in terms of where you live, the type of partner you prefer, how many children you have, the sport you play, how many hours you prefer to work, etc. These preferences do not usually change too much from young adulthood. By this stage, you have an innate sense of what you want, more or less.

3. Seek out people in your chosen career, doing what it is you envision for yourself; and speak to these people. Please, please, please do not ignore this step. It is one of the most important things you need to do when planning a career. Your image of the job and accompanying lifestyle may be very different from reality. You need to observe and note what these people's lives are like in terms of working hours, flexibility, demands, and challenges. What are the options for growth in the industry? Note, in particular, the following:

    • Can you open your own business in the field, and do you think you might want to? Alternatively, would you always be working for someone else?

    • Would it be possible to have flexible hours or work from home?

    • What is the pay like, when you start and ten or twenty years down the line?

    • What is the scope for promotions and career advancement?

    • What is it like for employees at the top of this profession? Do you see yourself living that way?
      Please add any and all relevant questions to this list and ensure that you get answers.

4. Correlate how you envision your life to be and the reality of the lifestyle that comes with the particular career choice.

This is crucially important. It is heartbreaking to spend five or ten years getting to the top of your career only to realise that you hate the lifestyle it brings. Please note that what you do while training and what you do once qualified and working may be very different.

Remember, also, that the drive to succeed and work hard is great when you are younger, which is good, but you need to know exactly where you are going. Your energy levels, priorities, and drive will not be the same in ten years' time. Your financial commitments and needs will also be very different. Please keep this in mind.

Just to give you an example, I started earning, after seven years of medical school and training, plus or minus R20,000 a month take-home in my own general medical practice (South African Rands currency which is the equivalent of approximately $1,363 American dollars). I thought at the time (in my mid-twenties) that this was great. Now, twenty years later, that salary doesn't even cover the interest on my home loan (the interest, not the instalment).

If you have to work hard initially and foresee yourself retiring when you are forty years old, that is great. Just remember to factor in exercise and a good lifestyle along the way. If you do decide to change career paths, that is fine. Every experience teaches you something. The only caveat is that you shouldn't lose too much of yourself or your health in the process.

An informed, well-thought-out decision is always a better one. You cannot plan for every eventuality or accurately predict the future (unless you are clairvoyant or really lucky). Considering all these factors can help you make the best decisions for you and those closest to you.

Although much of this may seem like common sense, it doesn't always play out that way. The euphoria from completing school and having the world at your feet can sometimes cloud the reality of twenty years down the line.

PERSONAL NOTES

PERSONAL NOTES

CHAPTER 12
SINGLE PARENT/ABSENT PARENT

If they answer not to your call walk alone …
If they shut doors and do not hold up the light
When the night is troubled with storm,
O thou unlucky one,
With the thunder flame of pain
Ignite your own heart,
And let it burn alone.
—'Ekla Chalo Re', Rabindranath Tagore

If you have grown up without one or both of your parents, please read this chapter very carefully. You are different: special, unique, and different. This is not a bad thing! When one or both parents are absent, for whatever duration of time in your life, it is impossible and unnatural for this not to impact on you in some way.

You watch the children around you while growing up and wonder what it would be like to have a mummy and daddy living together, loving each other and you. You would have nothing to worry about other than homework and friends. There would be no feeling responsible for your parent (if you have one) or guilt.

For children with an absent parent, there is always some sort of misbegotten guilt. You wonder if you might have done something to cause or aggravate this broken family situation or to warrant not having a parent or parents. What did you do to deserve this type of life? Children in such circumstances often lack the confidence that comes from knowing that you are loved unconditionally by both your parents. There is often a subconscious feeling of needing to prove that you are indeed good enough to deserve a family, to have a good life, and most of all, to be worthy of love and affection.

Sometimes this leads to unhealthy romantic relationships. It can also lead to striving to prove yourself academically and in other scenarios, which can be exhausting to the body, mind, and soul. Alternatively, it can lead to addiction to fill the void, apathy, or depression due to a lack of self-confidence. The desire to be a part of something and to belong somewhere can also be dangerous in certain social settings, such as where gangs and cults are prevalent.

Psychoanalysis of the abandoned child can go into many volumes, which you could research if you are so inclined. Most of us, however, don't realise all of these dynamics. We don't grow up with the psychotherapy we might have benefitted from because we are too busy trying to live with all the inherent challenges. There is also no insight on our part, or there may be a lack of financial means. We are merely innocent children believing that we are normal like everyone else because we want to fit in, not be some weird misfits.

Well, we are not entirely *normal* in many ways. My precious fellow friends, for the purposes of this book, and especially so that you may show the world what you have to offer, this is what I want you to know: You need to devote time to understanding yourself, your needs, and your dreams. This is really important because your subconscious has been bombarded with so many variables that you aren't even aware of.

Try to understand your motivation—why you do the things you do. Are you considering a particular career to prove something to the absent parent, to the world, to yourself, or is it what you really, truly want to do? If you have achieved great academic success, don't let this blind you into thinking that this is essentially what life is all about. It is not. There is so much more that you will only realise later in life because you have expended such a significant amount of your energy striving to prove yourself.

Now, you must just breathe, think, and explore all your options. If you have grown up with opportunities to see the world and all the opportunities available, then you are fortunate. If you have not, this is the time to do it. You can't choose appropriately if you don't know what your options are, and today the options are limitless.

Remember always that you are good enough and deserve to be successful, loved, and happy as much as anyone else. You do not have to prove yourself to be worthy of being loved and accepted. You don't need a career to prove this. You should choose a career that will make you happy and be fulfilling to your soul. It need not be a career filled with a huge amount of pomp and prestige. Choose from your heart and soul.

For those of you who feel guilty or inadequate, please stop. You have done nothing wrong. In fact, you are so strong and confident on a soul level that you chose the challenges you did for this lifetime to learn whatever lessons you needed to. It takes a courageous being to undertake a life on this planet without a parent. You are one formidable badass! You have got this! Furthermore, the insights and compassion that you have developed from growing up the way you did are an asset to the world.

People who don't go through the experience of abandonment will never understand what it's all about. The deep sense of understanding and empathy is not something you can learn from textbooks or movies. It's innate. It's a part of you, and it makes you powerful to be able to reach out and help people in ways that others can't.

This is why I feel it's so important for you to follow your heart and your soul's true purpose. Share your magic and power with the world.

The other potentially dangerous mindset that can arise from this type of background is that you indulge in self-pity and wither away, drowning your sorrows in some way or other. Please pull yourself up. Whatever the circumstances, this attitude will get you nowhere and accomplish nothing. You will be wasting this lifetime instead of learning from your experience and growing. Ultimately, that is what we are here for: to learn and grow, not be pampered and feed our egos. Don't be envious of those living that way. That's none of your concern. You have your own path. Make it count.

There may be a desire in you to fit in somewhere or be part of a family of some sort. You need to understand this so that you can keep it in perspective. There may be a yearning to be part of a family—perhaps a relative's or a friend's family—especially if you have no siblings. This can bring you much joy if others welcome you into their homes. It can also bring you much heartache.

It is wonderful to spend time with people and develop close relationships, but please try as much as possible not to have expectations. They are already a unit. As much as they may indulge you, there may come a point in time when you will feel like a total outsider. This can be very painful, as you feel things so much more strongly. Your abandonment issues also make you vulnerable, and it can be very harsh to your soul.

Remember that it isn't their fault. They are just functioning as a family. You have conjured up a lot more in your mind due to your loneliness and need to belong somewhere. You may also be more unconditionally loving and giving, so it is important to understand that not everyone can reciprocate this intensity of emotion and sincerity. You do not need to hide away from human relationships; just understand all the perspectives so that you know what to expect and can protect yourself to some extent.

You are special just as you are. If people can't accept you or understand you, move on. Don't try too hard to fit in anywhere. Rather, be around people who are a natural effortless fit. Focus on what's important to you. You are not alone in the world. Chase your dreams, focus on what makes you happy, and sooner or later, your tribe will find you. Your friendships or associations should be in harmony with your soul, uplifting, and compatible with making a positive impact on the world.

PERSONAL NOTES

PERSONAL NOTES

CHAPTER 13
YOUNG WOMEN: POINTS TO PONDER CAREFULLY

When you know and accept yourself without trying to be someone else, you can better decide what will and won't work for you. You will be the architect of your life instead of a passenger swept away at the mercy of the currents.

It is no secret that as women, our needs, especially at certain times in our lives, are very different from those of men. Our strengths and talents are also vastly different. To ignore that which makes us unique and special is a huge waste of potential. By acknowledging who you are—your strengths, weaknesses, needs, and attributes— you can understand yourself better. This will build confidence and help you make the best decisions for you.

Based on my careful and astute observation over the years, as well as personal experience, one of the vital factors that impacts a woman's choices in life is her confidence. When you know and accept yourself without trying to be someone else, you can better decide what will and won't work for you. You will be the architect of your life instead of a passenger swept away and at the mercy of the currents.

One of the key variables in life is your career. You should have your own money. If not, you compromise your degree of independence and personal power, which translates into life choices and personal freedom. I am not even going to entertain the option of marrying into money, as I do not consider this real financial security. It is fragile and fraught with insecurity on so many levels.

Preferably, make your own money and make sure no one can take it away from you.

Unless you have a huge inheritance or trust fund, chances are you will have to work for your money. What kind of career would you prefer? Do you see yourself as a corporate executive, attending meetings, managing people, and flying all over the world? Does this idea excite you? If so, great! Go for it! On the other hand, does the thought of not being home for dinner most nights or not being able to pick up your kids from school make you uncomfortable? Then this sort of high-flying career is probably not for you.

Do you expect your life partner to share the household chores and parenting responsibilities? Please do not take that for granted. Not everyone is on the same page with this. You need to talk about it. There is nothing whatsoever wrong with being a traditional housewife (with money of your own), if that is what you want. It is your choice. There is no single blueprint for everyone. This is why it is important to identify who you are and what your expectations are, not just out of life but also of your partner.

When we are young and the playing field is level, it is so easy to compete with the guys and beat them often. It gets a lot more complicated later on in life. Don't continuously strive to play by their rules. You will compromise your heart's true wishes and sell your soul. Just because you may be smarter or more skilful and deserving of that partnership or promotion does not mean that you must do everything in your power to get it. You do not need to prove anything to anyone. Know your worth.

It is unrealistic, cruel, and unfair to be expected to compete, especially in the corporate world, where the playing field is never level. If you have a family, you have to jump over hurdles and through hoops most men and single people can't even imagine. Once again, it's about confidence, understanding, and personal choice. If you don't want a family and children, then by all means, go ahead and compete. You will do great. If having children is important to you, please think long and hard.

You don't have to play by anyone else's rules, least of all those of the patriarchal, chauvinistic organizations of the world. There is the option of getting help with regard to school pickups, helping with homework, cooking, and so on in order to meet the demands of working life. There are also often options in the work environment that can give you more flexibility and autonomy over your time so that you can get a good balance between work and career—the type of balance that will suit you. Not everyone wants a fifty-fifty.

Personally, I value my quality time both with my kids and on my own. A good balance for me is about 20 per cent work, 60 per cent family, and 20 per cent personal time. You need to decide what your needs are. As I have discussed in more detail in the chapters on 'The Rest of Your Life', 'Children and Your Career', and 'Health and Career', only you will know this. It is more important for you as woman, though, because you have more parental responsibilities and your maternal instincts and needs are on a different level, which leaves you with less time for yourself. This is why it is so important for you to think carefully and know yourself well when choosing careers.

Please remember that you are not a robot, a clone of anyone, or a Stepford wife/employee/person. You are unique, capable, and most of all deserving of the best life for you. Only you can make it happen. Go for it!

PERSONAL NOTES

PERSONAL NOTES

CHAPTER 14
LAST WORDS:

1. Don't Be Afraid to Change Your Mind

It is never too late to be what you might have been.
—George Elliot

As beneficial as it may be to make the right career choice ab initio, it is not by any means a binding decision, cast in stone, regardless of what anyone tells you. Do not pressure yourself to make the right one now, if you are still not sure.

My intention with this book is to empower you as much as possible when you are choosing your career. It is not to fill you with anxiety when you already have enough to contend with. If, after reading all I've written and working through the exercises diligently, you are still unsure, that's just fine. If you have the option of a gap year, this could be extremely beneficial. It is something you will need to discuss with your parents.

Alternatively, you could choose the option most suitable to your character and needs, and keep an open mind. You can always change course at a later stage. Be vigilant over your thoughts and feelings. Ask yourself often along the way how you feel about your chosen path (this applies to general aspects of life as well). Don't be scared to change, as long as your financial obligations and dependents are taken care of. You must set a viable, sensible course. Careful planning is essential.

2. Save

> The art is not in making money but in keeping it.
> —Proverb

Whatever it is you choose to do with your life, from the moment you start earning, please, please save. Consider the following ways to put money aside:

- **Retirement planning**: Start doing this as soon as you start earning money.
- **Medical aid/medical insurance**: Unless you live in a country with excellent public healthcare, insurance is an absolute, non-negotiable necessity. Please ensure that you and your family are adequately covered.
- **Special funds**: In addition to retirement and medical aid, you should have a fund to function as a safety net. This is to cover you just in case you can't work for a while, or if you decide to change careers. If the Corona Virus/COVID-19 Pandemic (2019 Onset) has taught us anything, it is how unpredictable life can be. When it comes to finances and health this can have devastating consequences. My advice is that you aim to have at least one year of your salary as savings. This will help see you through until you are earning well again. To accomplish this, when you start working, don't change your lifestyle too much, until you've saved enough money to be able to live comfortably, were you not able to work for a year. Just hold out on that car upgrade and home for a little longer. Off course, having more than one year's earnings in salary is even better, but not always possible. Just be practical and sensible. Furthermore, don't spend this money, unless it's absolutely necessary.
- **Professional provident fund**: This is a policy that covers you financially if you get sick. It is optional and especially

pertinent to those who do not have large monetary reserves to fall back on.

- **Holiday fund**: This one is my favourite. It is always a good idea. Everyone needs a good holiday at least once a year. It need not be a huge amount. Just put away a little every month, according to what you can afford. It really does help, and it gives you something wonderful to look forward to at least once a year.

3. Do Not Compromise Your Health

I have already touched on this, but I feel compelled to emphasize it again, hopefully for effect. Your health and well-being, physically and spiritually, are your greatest asset and wealth in this lifetime. Do not take it for granted. Protect it with all you have.

Smoking is more dangerous than you can ever imagine. The consequences for your body range from a huge increased incidence of cancer (not just lung cancer) to respiratory effects and cardiac problems. It is an evil beyond words. Do not start, or stop if you already have. Research it to get a more comprehensive idea.

Drugs are the scourge of society. Too many young people have destroyed their lives or died because of this evil. Stay away. You may feel just one time won't do any harm. That's how every drug addict gets started. It will destroy you and your family. If you need a high, find a better one. Sport is the most beneficial, and the endorphins are wonderful for your body and mind.

Alcohol is an insidious evil with far-reaching, irreversible effects. I have watched it destroy so many lives, including many within my own family. Wonderful, high-functioning people have succumbed. You have worked too hard and have too much to offer the world to throw it all away senselessly.

With all of these evils, you will think you have it under control. You will feel you are too smart to let it control you. You will believe that you are in charge, just having a bit of harmless fun. That's the secret and power of the beast. It lulls you into a false sense of security, works through your ego by making you feel amazing, and then rips you to shreds before you know it. Many of the effects cannot be undone. No amount of money can bring back your health when it's lost. You risk your family, close friends, health—everything.

Exercise

I cannot stress enough how important a good fitness routine is. This will improve or maintain great health, mentally and physically, in every possible way. The benefits are limitless, from preventing heart disease, diabetes, and dementia to improving your skin and general quality of life.

Yoga and Meditation

Aside from the benefits to your mind and body, these activities are your connection to the divine. We often pray to God, but do we listen to the answers? Life gets so crazy that we hardly ever take the time to reflect and listen to the guidance from within and the cosmic powers that be. Regular yoga practices have shown to improve and even cure medical ailments that medicine and science have failed to relieve, including many cases of rheumatoid arthritis. This is coming from a medical doctor, so you should heed the advice.

4. Beware of Name Brands

Be very careful and aware of the allure of name-brand items, especially clothing, and of living to impress others. When you start earning, you will be tempted by all sorts of luxuries. Media and marketing are a powerful force; they make you believe that you desperately need things you may not even have known existed. Things you really don't need.

Remember always that what you have in your heart, mind, and soul far surpass any benefit material things can give you. Your true worth is within you. We come into the world alone, and we leave alone. All the material acquisitions are for this world only. By all means, enjoy the wealth and prosperity you have earned, but keep it in perspective. Wonderful life experiences—travel, relationships, education (all types), spiritual growth—will enhance your spirit and be part of you forever. The fancy handbag won't!

You don't need brand-name items to define you or give you status. If it's for comfort or performance, and you can afford it without compromising other important areas of your life, then by all means, enjoy it. Please do not live outside of your means or by just getting through in order to impress anyone. People who truly care about you will not care about what you wear, what you drive, or where you live. Do those other people really matter?

Don't let the trappings of wealth and good fortune shackle you in any way. Live light and free, with enough money saved to give yourself choices in terms of career, the country you live in, travel opportunities and such. Remember always that the best things in life are free.

PERSONAL NOTES

PERSONAL NOTES

ABOUT THE AUTHOR

So then, finally, who am I and why did I write this book? Just in case you were wondering.

When I finished school, I was one of the top students in my country (South Africa). The world was my oyster. My first choice, in line with my aptitude and proclivities, was actuarial science; however, this necessitated moving to another province to study. My mum was a single parent, and I grew up in a traditional family where medicine was held in high regard. The thought of entering unchartered territory (which actuarial science was at that time) was rather daunting, so I chose the tried and tested 'safe' path.

I hated medical school, but I persevered, being determined, smart, and not one to back down from a challenge. This thing would not break me! It was also a case of wanting to prove myself and not having the financial backup to change course midway. I already had student loans looming over me.

I qualified as a doctor and subsequently specialized to become an Anatomical Pathologist. I also attained an MBA degree, and half a BCom degree along the way. As a pathologist, I currently look at slides of tissue specimens under a microscope to make diagnoses. For example, if someone has a breast mass, the surgeon will remove it and send it to my laboratory. We then cut the tissue into smaller pieces and process it through various stages, resulting in a slide with the tissue on it. I then look at it under the microscope, send a report to the surgeon describing the tissue, and let him know the diagnosis (whether it's a malignant or benign tumour, an abscess, or something else). It is a noble path and an honest, respected job for which I am extremely grateful. However, I cannot help wondering what could have been. It is a job, and like so many of my colleagues, I have reached a stage in my life where I want to do something else.

There is no doubt that there will be people, even after reading this book, who at some point in their lives might want to change paths. That is fine. Our personalities and needs change as we go through life. What I want is for everyone reading this book to have access to as much information as possible. Even if you do decide to change paths, you must be empowered by understanding what's going on in your mind. You would benefit greatly by taking into consideration everything discussed in this book.

I've made mistakes personally and professionally in terms of choices that were less than ideal. Choices that stemmed from an innate sense of insecurity, a need for recognition, acceptance, and validation of my worth. The underlying cause of all this is beyond the intended scope of this book. Let it suffice to say that whatever the demons of our individual pasts, we need not be bound and defined by them. Yes, if necessary, please explore the root of your angst and torment to understand yourself better and heal from it. Do not, I implore you, dwell on it obsessively or on the people involved. That will just hamper your progress in this lifetime. Forgive whatever needs to be forgiven. It will lessen your burden and free you to be the best version of yourself.

I wish for you to make wiser choices for yourself. I did not understand myself and my needs very well as a young person. What works for others will not necessarily work for you or me. Only you can make the best choices for you, and only when those choices come from a place of confidence, a strong sense of self-worth, understanding, and a degree of knowledge.

You must start thinking about all the facts, issues, and variables involved. This will help you understand yourself better and your motivation for your choices. You can then regroup within yourself (however many times necessary in your lifetime) to make better decisions. This can only happen from a position of power and security, not from the position of an insecure child.

You deserve to be happy. Focus on what makes you happy— the you who has accepted the past, grown from it, and is ready to move on to the beautiful future that awaits. Yes, ultimately it is that simple. Sometimes we complicate our lives by placing too much significance on other variables, including status, wealth, and our personal perceptions of circumstances that have held us back. The personal benefits from choices made purely for the gain of wealth and status are short-lived. They do not bring fulfilment and happiness in the long term.

Remember always that knowledge is power. Knowing yourself well is the ultimate power. No one will be able to lead you astray, however well-meaning they may be. My hope and vision is to empower you to be the best you can be in this life. Yes, it is a journey, not a destination, but having the advantages of correct gear and knowledge certainly will help.

Good luck and God bless!

APPENDIX 1
SOME OF MY FAVOURITE BOOKS

- *A Little Light on the Spiritual Laws* by Diana Cooper
- *Losing My Virginity* by Sir Richard Branson
- *Spiritual Growth* by Sanaya Roman
- *Autobiography of a Yogi* by Paramhansa Yogananda
- *Long Walk to Freedom* by Nelson R. Mandela
- *The Last Lecture* by Randy Pausch
- *The Power of Now* by Eckhart Tolle
- *If I Could Tell You Just One Thing* by Richard Reed
- *The Monk Who Sold His Ferrari* by Robin Sharma
- *Whispers from Eternity* by Paramhansa Yogananda
- *Big Magic* by Elizabeth Gilbert
- *Broken Open* by Elizabeth Lesser
- *Disappearance of the Universe* by Gary Renard.

APPENDIX 2
NOTES TO PARENTS

Your children are not your children.
They are the sons and daughters of Life's longing for itself.
They come through you but not from you,
And though they are with you yet they belong not to you.
You may give them your love but not your thoughts,
For they have their own thoughts.
You may house their bodies but not their souls,
For their souls dwell in the house of tomorrow,
Which you cannot visit, not even in your dreams.
You may strive to be like them,
But seek not to make them like you.
For life goes not backward nor tarries with yesterday.

—Kahlil Gibran, The Prophet

As the first source of guidance, inspiration, and security, parents play a crucial role in their children's lives. Your children trust you and look to you for guidance. It is therefore imperative that you are careful in the way you treat your children and the things you say and do.

You need to think about what sort of role you want to play in your child's life. If it's really and truly the child's decision, then as a parent, you need to be vigilant regarding how you react to everything career-related. The following three basic rules apply here:

1. Do not manipulate the young child/young adult. This means do not pass snide remarks or make the child feel guilty for making any particular decision.
2. Do not try to influence the child one way or another.

3. Stay neutral. Expose your child to as much information and knowledge as you can, but don't be biased.

If you find yourself unable to support your child's career choice, admit this to yourself. Acknowledge it. Ask yourself why you are being this way and if it's worth it. Is it so important for you to oppose this? Why? Is it for your ego, comfort, or other people's opinions and approval?

If you are sick, elderly, or have special needs of any sort and would prefer for your child to live close by, acknowledge this and consider options that will not derail your child's dreams. Can you get relatives or hire someone to help you out? Can you move closer to your child's tertiary centre? If these are not practical options, then perhaps you can plan well for the future.

Discuss the options openly with your child. You can, perhaps, save over the next few years or months. In that time, perhaps the course can be done part-time if possible, then converted to full-time studies. Alternatively, you could hire someone to help out for now, and when your child qualifies, then you can review the situation. If it's a question of insufficient funds, the options include getting a loan, applying for a bursary from a relevant institution (bank or private company in the field), studying part-time through correspondence, or working full-time until enough funds are available to do the course.

If you could manage on your own but would rather not, consider if it's worth possibly ruining your child's future for your own selfish reasons. Remember, you do not own your children. It was your choice to have them. It is not fair to make them feel obligated to you at this early, crucial stage in their lives, irrespective of your circumstances and challenges. If you really love them, you will do what is best for them.

Children are extremely vulnerable and easily influenced due to their need or desire to please you and gain your approval, especially if you've been harsh, critical, and disapproving of them or their behaviour in the past. This is an opportunity for them to get your approval or to please you with their decision. This is the emotional state of many teenagers at some point.

Even if your children seem exceptionally mature, confident, and totally responsible, they are still children on the brink of adulthood. Please do not manipulate this innocence and vulnerability for your own selfish reasons. It is not your right. It is your responsibility to raise them, feed them, and educate them. They do not owe you their entire future.

Make a concerted effort to avoid saying things like, 'It's your choice. You can do whatever you like, but it would be nice if you decided …' That is not on! It will play on their minds and rack them with guilt. If it's truly their choice, you will not manipulate them, subtly or overtly. It is still manipulation, and it's not acceptable.

Confidence and Self-Worth

There is a great misconception that confidence and self-worth go hand in hand. They do not. Brilliant academics or accomplished athletes may be extremely confident in those abilities, but this does not necessarily mean they feel a sense of worthiness in their heart and soul. Self-worth is an intricate and complex aspect of our nature. It is built over time, starting in childhood. A person who has been constantly criticised, chastised, and rejected will find it very difficult to feel the degree of self-worth that a person who has grown up with unconditional love, encouragement, and support does.

Be careful with your criticism. Do not compare children, and do not have ridiculous expectations. Being strict and well-disciplined is one thing. Breaking a child's spirit and sabotaging that child's right to childhood is another. If you can't find a good balance, show more love and support. It will be far more beneficial to their confidence and self-worth. These are personality traits and assets that are very difficult to cultivate in adulthood when conquering deep-rooted scars and emotional trauma from childhood.

One's sense of self-worth—more, I believe, than confidence—impacts on many life decisions, including the choice of romantic partners. A strong sense of self-worth will protect individuals from accepting less than they deserve from a partner. They will be far less likely to tolerate abuse of any sort and will make better decisions personally and professionally because they know at their core that they are worthy of the best life they can have.

The Rest of Your Child's Life

I feel compelled at this point to discuss your attitude as a parent towards other aspects of your children's lives, whether they are young children or adults. Your attitude and comments regarding gender roles in a home with regard to housework, cooking, raising of children, and parental responsibilities are extremely important and can profoundly impact your children in their adult lives. An attitude of shared responsibility in all household activities and parental duties will go a long way in helping them as adults, irrespective of whether they are boys or girls,

If you wish for your children to have happy and successful lives, not just successful and lucrative careers, then don't fill their heads with unrealistic fairy-tale expectations. Listen to how they feel and what they need. What worked for you may not necessarily work for them, so please don't impose your philosophy of life onto them. Raising a family and maintaining a home should be a shared responsibility, and how they decide to determine each one's role is up to them. Different roles work in different families, but it is entirely up to the individuals involved to decide on this.

Marriage is not a necessity. Do not ever pressure anyone into it in any way. In many instances, there is a great emphasis on academia and career, almost to the exclusion of all else. Then suddenly, once this is on track, the emphasis shifts to marriage and children. Unfortunately, the bulk of the responsibility in this area still falls on the woman's shoulders. Needless to say, without careful planning and understanding the inherent demands, this can be a completely overwhelming and daunting experience, with potentially hazardous effects on a woman's mental and physical health.

On the other hand, there is no such thing that the man of the house needs to earn more, or have a more prestigious job. These ideas result in unnecessary pressure and have a subconscious mental effect, which could adversely impact his relationships especially if his partner is earning more, or is more highly qualified than he is. Men are also perfectly capable of caring for children, and yes, it is their responsibility as much as their partners.

As a parent, you can prepare your children for their future challenges by being honest, candid, supportive, and loving. Promote equality and fairness in all ways. Chauvinism starts in the home, in childhood. It needs to stop for the benefit of both husbands and wives. If people understand from childhood that both genders are equal in all aspects, it will be a natural progression to adulthood. This will go a long way to ensuring happy, healthy relationships.

Printed in the United States
By Bookmasters